LITERATURE AND CRITICAL THINKING
Art Projects•Bulletin Boards•Plot Summaries
Skill Building Activities•Independent Thinking

Written by: John & Patty Carratello
Illustrated by: Theresa Wright

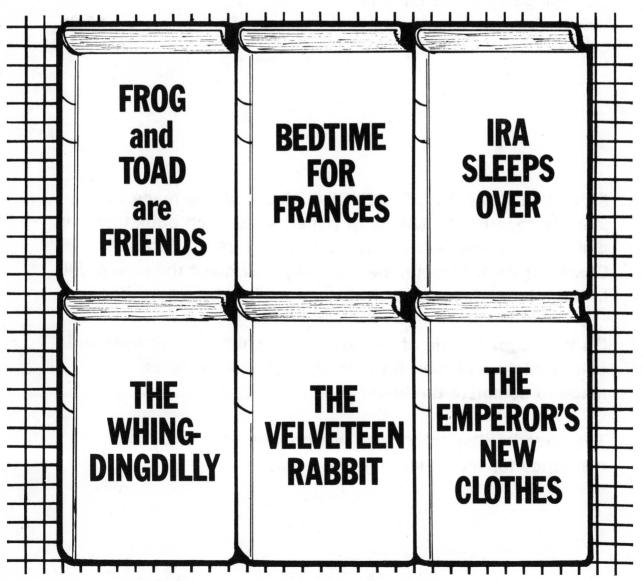

FROG and TOAD are FRIENDS

BEDTIME FOR FRANCES

IRA SLEEPS OVER

THE WHING-DINGDILLY

THE VELVETEEN RABBIT

THE EMPEROR'S NEW CLOTHES

Teacher Created Materials

Teacher Created Materials, Inc.
P. O. Box 1214
Huntington Beach, CA 92649
© Teacher Created Materials, Inc. 1987
Made in U.S.A.
ISBN 1-55734-356-X

TABLE OF CONTENTS

FAVORITE CHARACTER MEMORY BOOK can be made by stapling together 12 sheets of paper. After each book unit, the children may select one character to receive the Favorite Character Award from page 78. They may color the award, fill in the information and paste the award in their award book.

On the opposite side of the paper, the children can draw and color a picture of their favorite character. A cover can be made to complete the book.

The Favorite Character Book will provide very enjoyable memories for the children in the future.

INTRODUCTION

LITERATURE FOR CRITICAL THINKING

It is possible for all children at varying developmental levels to engage in a discovery process which clarifies thinking, increases knowledge, and deepens their understanding of human issues and social values. This activities book, based on Bloom's *Taxonomy of Skills in the Cognitive Domain,* provides teachers a resource to maximize this process, using distinguished children's literature as a vehicle.

The authors suggest the following options in using this book:

OPTION 1: The teacher may select a single activity for the entire class.

OPTION 2: The teacher may select different activities for single students or small groups of students.

OPTION 3: The student may select the level he or she wishes to work at, once the teacher explains what is available.

The stories in this book follow the same format, so that each level of thinking skills is approached as follows:

KNOWLEDGE

This level provides the child with an opportunity to recall fundamental facts and information about the story. Success at this level will be evidenced by the child's ability to:

Activity 1: Match character names with pictures of the characters.

Activity 2: Identify the main characters in a crossword puzzle.

Activity 3: Match statements with the characters who said them.

Activity 4: List the main characteristics of one of the main characters in a WANTED poster.

Activity 5: Arrange scrambled story pictures in sequential order.

Activity 6: Arrange scrambled story sentences in sequential order.

Activity 7: Recall details about the setting by creating a picture of where a part of the story took place.

COMPREHENSION

This level provides the child with an opportunity to demonstrate a basic understanding of the story. Success at this level will be evidenced by the child's ability to:

Activity 1: Interpret pictures of scenes from the story.

Activity 2:	Explain selected ideas or parts from the story in his or her own words.
Activity 3:	Draw a picture showing what happened before and after a passage or illustration found in the book.
Activity 4:	Write a sentence explaining what happened before and after a passage or illustration found in the book.
Activity 5:	Predict what *could* happen next in the story before the reading of the entire book is completed.
Activity 6:	Construct a pictorial time line which summarizes what happens in the story.
Activity 7:	Explain how the main character felt at the beginning, middle, and/or end of the story.

APPLICATION

This level provides the child with an opportunity to use information from the story in a new way. Success at this level will be evidenced by the child's ability to:

Activity 1:	Classify the characters as human, animal, or thing.
Activity 2:	Transfer a main character to a new setting.
Activity 3:	Make finger puppets and act out a part of the story.
Activity 4:	Select a meal that one of the main characters would enjoy eating, plan a menu, and a method of serving it.
Activity 5:	Think of a situation that occurred to a character in the story and write about how he or she would have handled the situation differently.
Activity 6:	Give examples of people the child knows who have the same problems as the characters in the story.

ANALYSIS

This level provides the child with an opportunity to take parts of the story and examine these parts carefully in order to better understand the whole story. Success at this level will be evidenced by the child's ability to:

Activity 1:	Identify general characteristics (stated and/or implied) of the main characters.
Activity 2:	Distinguish what could happen from what couldn't happen in the story in real life.
Activity 3:	Select parts of the story that were funniest, saddest, happiest, and most unbelievable.
Activity 4:	Differentiate fact from opinion.
Activity 5:	Compare and/or contrast two of the main characters.
Activity 6:	Select an action of a main character that was exactly the same as something the child would have done.

SYNTHESIS

This level provides the child with an opportunity to put parts from the story together in a new way to form a new idea or product. Success at this level will be evidenced by the child's ability to:

Activity 1: Create a story from just the title *before* the story is read (pre-story exercise).

Activity 2: Write three new titles for the story that would give a good idea what it was about.

Activity 3: Create a poster to advertise the story so people will want to read it.

Activity 4: Create a new product related to the story.

Activity 5: Restructure the roles of the main characters to create new outcomes in the story.

Activity 6: Compose and perform a dialogue or monologue that will communicate the thoughts of the main character(s) at a given point in the story.

Activity 7: Imagine that he or she is one of the main characters and write a diary account of daily thoughts and activities.

Activity 8: Create an original character and tell how the character would fit into the story.

Activity 9: Write the lyrics and music to a song that one of the main characters would sing if he/she/it became a rock star — and perform it.

EVALUATION

This level provides the child with an opportunity to form and present an opinion backed up by sound reasoning. Success at this level will be evidenced by the child's ability to:

Activity 1: Decide which character in the selection he or she would most like to spend a day with and why.

Activity 2: Judge whether or not a character should have acted in a particular way and why.

Activity 3: Decide if the story really could have happened and justify reasons for decision.

Activity 4: Consider how this story can help the child in his or her own life.

Activity 5: Appraise the value of the story.

Activity 6: Compare this story with another one the child has read.

Activity 7: Write a recommendation as to why the book should be read or not.

In addition to the activities just outlined, a class project and a small groups project will be included for each story.

Bedtime For Frances

by Russell Hoban

It is time for a little badger named Frances to go to bed. Her mother and father give her a glass of milk, tuck her in with a bear and a doll, and kiss her several times. But Frances can't sleep. Imagining there are tigers and giants in her room, she leaves her bed to seek her parents' comfort. Not surprisingly, she also finds it necessary to eat a piece of cake, brush her teeth, and do a number of other things that will postpone her sleep. Her father responds sensitively to her needs and fears at first, but finally insists upon bedtime with the threat of a spanking. With that, Frances finally settles down and goes to sleep.

SCRAMBLED EXCUSES

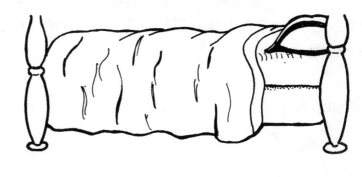

Here is a list of five excuses Frances made for not going to bed and staying there. Which order did they happen in the story? Write them in the order Frances used them.

1. "Something scary is going to come out of the crack in the ceiling."

2. "The giant wants to get me."

3. "There is something moving the curtains."

4. "I want a glass of milk."

5. "There is a tiger in my room."

Write the excuses in order here.

1. _____
   _____

2. _____
   _____

3. _____
   _____

4. _____
   _____

5. _____

THE GIANT!

Frances saw something big and dark in her room. She thought it was a giant. Was it?_____

Draw a picture of the "giant" Frances thought she saw.

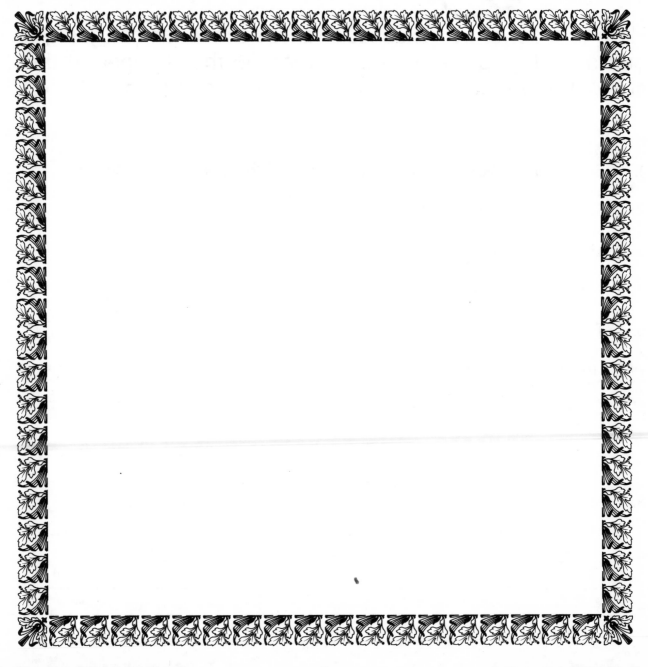

8

WAKE UP!

Pretend you are **Frances**. Explain what is happening in this picture. Remember to explain it like **Frances** would.

_____

_____

_____

_____

_____

Pretend you are **Father**. Explain what is happening in this picture. Remember to explain it like **Father** would.

_____

_____

_____

_____

FATHER KNOWS WHY

Father gave Frances answers for the things she said kept her awake. What did Father tell Frances after she said each of these things to him?

1. "There is a tiger in my room." _____

_____

_____

_____

2. "There is a giant in my room." _____

_____

_____

_____

3. "Something scary is going to come out of the crack in the ceiling." _____

_____

_____

_____

4. "There is something moving the curtains." _____

_____

_____

_____

NO SCHOOL!

Frances was just awakened by her mother. She has now decided that she does not want to go to school. Using what you know about how Frances can make excuses, write five reasons why she says, "I can't go to school."

1. _____
   _____

2. _____
   _____

3. _____
   _____

4. _____
   _____

5. _____
   _____

Using what you know about Frances and her parents, write what her mother or father might say to her as she gives one of the excuses you wrote for her.
Excuse number _____.

Mother or father's answer: _____

_____

_____

_____

_____

BUT I'M NOT SLEEPY!

Frances made excuses for not going to bed. Her parents were very patient with her excuses until the end. Write something that her parents might have said to each of these excuses if they had not been so patient.

1. "There is a tiger in my room." _____

_____

_____

_____

2. "May I have some cake?" _____

_____

_____

_____

3. "Something scary is going to come out of the crack in the ceiling." _____

_____

_____

_____

UNBELIEVABLE!

Frances made a lot of excuses for not going to bed and staying in bed. Some of the excuses she made show that she likes to imagine things that are not real.

Write three excuses Frances made that could not possibly be real.

1. _____

   _____

   _____

2. _____

   _____

   _____

3. _____

   _____

   _____

Now, on the back of this paper, draw **one** of these things that she imagined!

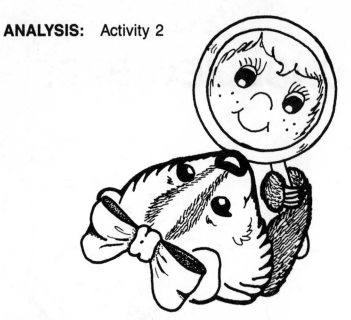

ME TOO!

Frances makes excuses for not going to bed.

1. Do **you** make excuses for not going to bed like Frances does? _____

2. What is one excuse for not going to bed that Frances uses that **you** would use also? _____
_____
_____

3. Do you think it would work with **your** parents? _____
Why?_____
_____
_____

Frances has fears about going to bed.

1. Do **you** have any fears about going to bed like Frances does? _____

2. What is one fear that Frances has that **you** have also? _____
_____
_____

3. Do you think **your** parents would understand your fear?_____
Why?_____
_____
_____

ALPHABET SONG

Read the alphabet song Frances sang again. It's your turn to make an alphabet song like hers! Work in groups of three or four. Complete the alphabet song on these lines. Then read or sing your group song to the class!

A is for _____

B is for _____

C is for _____

D is for _____

E is for _____

F is for _____

G is for _____

H is for _____

I is for _____

J is for _____

K is for _____

L is for _____

M is for _____

N is for _____

O is for _____

P is for _____

Q is for _____

R is for _____

S is for _____

T is for _____

U is for _____

V is for _____

W is for _____

X is for _____

Y is for _____

Z is for _____

GET IN BED!

Write one excuse that **you** use for not going to bed on time.

_____

_____

Raise your hand and share your excuses with the class. Your teacher will write all the excuses you and your classmates give, and number each one. Try to think of more excuses to share, too!

Your teacher will give you the number of one or more excuses to copy from the board. Copy it in this square. Color the border of the square and cut it out.

Help your teacher make a large bed from construction paper for a bulletin board. You and the rest of your classmates put all your excuse squares together to form a patchwork quilt of excuses to cover the bed!

EXCUSE NUMBER _____

The reason I can't go to bed and stay there is because_____

_____

_____

_____

_____

_____

_____

                              16

THINK ABOUT IT!

1. Why did Father finally say he would spank Frances if she didn't stay in bed? _____
   _____
   _____
   _____
   _____
   _____

2. Does Father love Frances? _____ How do you know?
   _____
   _____
   _____
   _____

3. Do you think Frances will have trouble going to sleep again? _____
   Why?_____
   _____
   _____
   _____
   _____

WHAT WE LIKE MOST. . .

What would the following people like most about **Bedtime for Frances?**

1. Your friends: _____

   _____

   _____

   Why? _____

   _____

2. Your parents: _____

   _____

   _____

   Why? _____

   _____

3. Your brother or sister: _____

   _____

   _____

   Why? _____

   _____

4. What did **you** like the most about the story? _____

   _____

   _____

   Why? _____

   _____

18

The Emperor's New Clothes

by Hans Christian Andersen

There was once an Emperor who was very fond of clothes. Spending time in his wardrobe was what he liked to do best. Then one day two tricksters arrived who pretended to be weavers. They said that they could weave a very special cloth that gave clothes made from it the quality of being invisible to those who were either unfit for their jobs or extremely stupid.

Intrigued by the prospect of having such clothes, the Emperor had the weavers begin work. Yet, as they worked, no onlooker would admit that he or she could not see the imaginary cloth—not even the Emperor! Instead, everyone praised the pattern and admired the colors of the cloth. Even the people of the city, not wanting to be found unfit or stupid, admired the Emperor's new clothes made from the special cloth as he paraded in a grand street procession. That is, until one little boy pointed out, "He has nothing on!"

Crossword Puzzle

In **The Emperor's New Clothes,** there are some words that may be new to you. To help you get to know these words better, here is a special crossword puzzle. Use a dictionary, along with the wordbox at the bottom of this page, to help you in finding the answers.

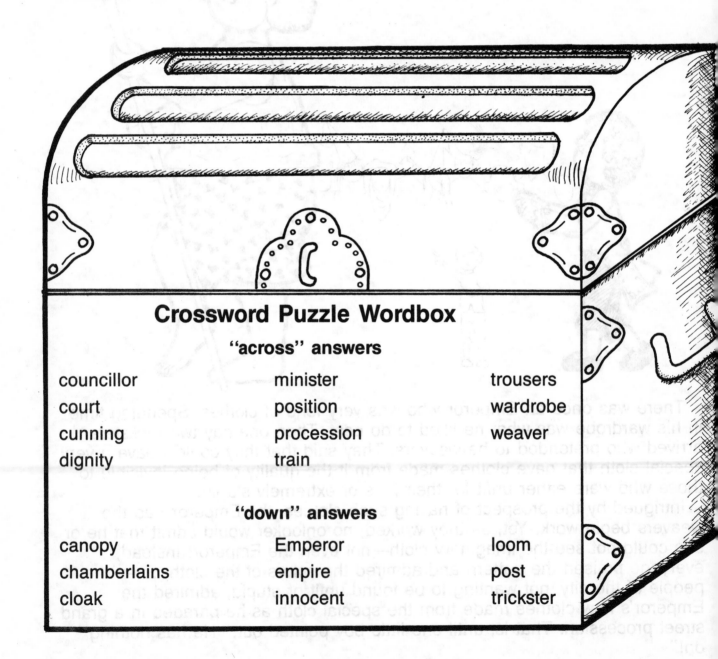

Crossword Puzzle Wordbox

"across" answers

councillor	minister	trousers
court	position	wardrobe
cunning	procession	weaver
dignity	train	

"down" answers

canopy	Emperor	loom
chamberlains	empire	post
cloak	innocent	trickster

Crossword Puzzle

across

2.   person who gives advice — c _ _ _ _ _ _ _ _ _ _
4.   person who makes cloth on a loom — w _ _ _ _ _ _
7.   a person's clothes — w _ _ _ _ _ _ _ _
9.   another name for pants — t_ _ _ _ _ _ _ _
10. a kind of parade — p _ _ _ _ _ _ _ _ _
12. a part of clothing that trails behind the person who wears it — t_ _ _ _ _
13. person who carries out the orders of another — m _ _ _ _ _ _ _ _
15. job — p_ _ _ _ _ _ _ _
16. the palace of a ruler like the Emperor and the people in it — c _ _ _ _ _
17. clever — c _ _ _ _ _ _
18. pride and self-respect — d _ _ _ _ _ _ _

down

1.   a machine for weaving thread or yarn into cloth — l _ _ _ _
2.   the Emperor's servants — c _ _ _ _ _ _ _ _ _ _ _ _ _
3.   like a cape — c _ _ _ _ _
5.   the ruler of an empire — E _ _ _ _ _ _ _
6.   the land ruled by an Emperor — e_ _ _ _ _ _ _
8.   job, another word for 15 across — p _ _ _ _
9.   a person who tricks — t_ _ _ _ _ _ _
11. a cover held on poles over a person — c _ _ _ _ _
14. a simple, honest person — i_ _ _ _ _ _ _ _

Wanted!

Make a wanted poster for the tricksters! Draw a picture of each one and fill in the blanks.

WANTED!

Trickster 1   Trickster 2

They are wanted by the Emperor because

_____

_____

_____

_____

_____

_____

_____

_____

_____

_____

What's Happening?

Color this picture. Then write a summary about what is happening in the picture on the lines below.

Summary

_____

_____

_____

_____

_____

_____

_____

How Do You Feel, Emperor?

1. How does the Emperor feel in the beginning of the story as he looks at his clothes?

    _____

    _____

    _____

    _____

    _____

    _____

2. How does the Emperor feel in the middle of the story when he can't see the tricksters' cloth?

    _____

    _____

    _____

    _____

    _____

    _____

3. How does the Emperor feel at the end of the story when the boy points out that the Emperor has no clothes on?

    _____

    _____

    _____

    _____

    _____

Sales Pitch!

A sales pitch is what someone says to convince you to buy something. In the story the tricksters convinced the Emperor to buy their clothes, even though we don't know exactly what they said to convince him. What do you think the tricksters said to the Emperor and what do you think he said to them? You decide! Talk it out!

DIRECTIONS:

1. Work in a group of three.
2. Decide who will be Trickster 1, Trickster 2 and the Emperor.
3. Assemble **your** character's finger puppet. Color and cut out your puppet. Paste top and bottom tabs together to form a loop that fits over your finger.
4. Work together to write dialogue for your sales pitch.
5. Memorize and practice your written dialogue.
6. Present your sales pitch to the class.

Emperor

Trickster 1

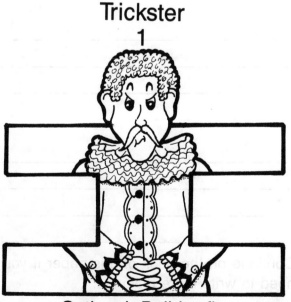

Trickster 2

Optional: Build a finger puppet stage out of a box for your group.

Dialogue

Trickster 1: _____

_____

_____

_____

_____

Trickster 2: _____

_____

_____

_____

_____

Emperor: _____

_____

_____

_____

_____

Trickster 1: _____

_____

_____

_____

_____

Trickster 2: _____

_____

_____

_____

Emperor: _____

_____

_____

_____

Continue on the back of this paper if you need to write more dialogue.

26

Just Fooling!

In the story, the Emperor and the people of the city were fooled by the two tricksters. Have you ever been fooled before?

_____

Write about a time when someone had wanted to fool you, to have you believe that something was true that really wasn't. Answer these questions.

1. Who wanted to fool you? _____

   _____

   _____

   _____

2. Why did he or she want to fool you? _____

   _____

   _____

   _____

3. What did that person do to fool you? _____

   _____

   _____

   _____

4. Were you actually fooled? _____ Why? _____

   _____

   _____

   _____

ANALYSIS: Activity 1

To Be Continued!

You have just finished reading **The Emperor's New Clothes.** What do you think might happen next if the story had not ended? Draw a picture and write about what you think might happen next. You may write on the back of this paper if you need more space.

The Emperor, Continued

_____

_____

_____

_____

Figure It Out!

Read both definitions given for each word. Select the definition that best describes the character or characters in the picture to the right of the word. Color the pictures. Then, recopy the correct definition on the lines below.

1. **vain** (vān) adj.

1. worthless. 2. caring too much about how one looks.

_____

_____

2. **crooked** (krook´id) adj.

1. dishonest. 2. not straight

_____

_____

3. **candid** (kan´did) adj.

1. very honest in what one says.
2. informal.

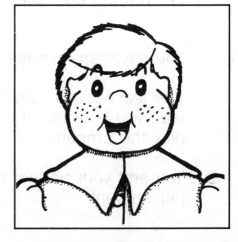

_____

_____

Talk Fast!

What if the Emperor's soldiers had caught the two tricksters trying to leave the city after the Emperor found out what they did?

What if you were one of the tricksters?

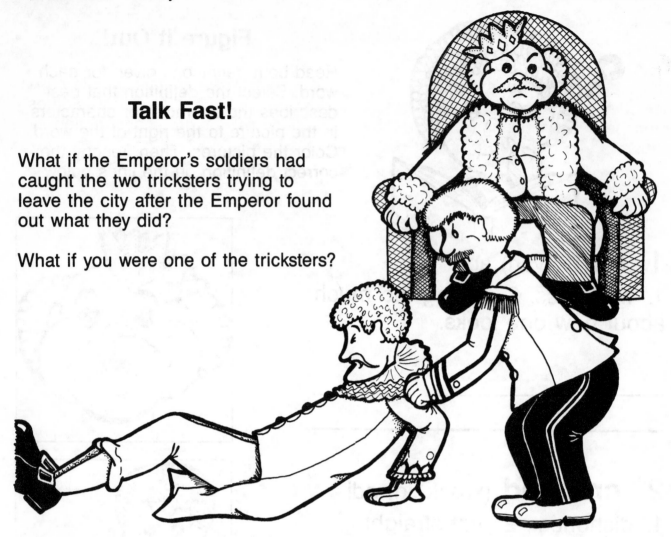

DIRECTIONS:

1. You will work with a partner in your class who will be the other trickster. Decide what you both will tell the Emperor when you are brought before him. Build your story around one of the following reasons:

   a) You really meant no harm.

   b) It was just a joke.

   c) You did it for the Emperor's own good.

   You have ten minutes to prepare. Make sure you both share the talking.

2. The teacher will select two or more students to be the guards who will lead you both into the palace. The teacher will also select a student to play the Emperor.

3. You and your partner must convince the Emperor to spare you from punishment!

New Tailor!

You are the Emperor's new tailor. You know how to make clothes people can see! Design clothes for him to wear to a party and to bed. Design the clothes over these Emperor figures. You may wish to use yarn, glitter, construction paper, fabric, or other things in your clothes designs.

Cover Up!

People do not want others to think they are stupid. So, to keep others from thinking they are stupid, they sometimes "cover up!" They say they know something that they really don't know or have done something they have never really done. That is, they tell a lie!

Have you ever covered up? Have you ever told a lie to someone about something so he or she wouldn't think you were stupid?

PROJECT: For one week, keep a daily record of all your cover ups. Your teacher will give you time every day to work on your record. Be sure to write **every** cover up that happens — at home or at school.

Cover Up	Reason for Cover Up
I said I was sick last night.	*Because* I didn't do my homework.
I said_____	Because_____
I said_____	Because_____
I said_____	Because_____
I said_____	Because_____

32

Looks!

The Emperor spent most of his time concerned about how he looked.

1. Do you think someone should spend most of his or her time thinking about how he or she looks? _____
    Why?_____
    _____
    _____
    _____
    _____

2. Do you care about how **you** look? _____ Why? _____
    _____
    _____
    _____
    _____
    _____

Think about it:

   If someone gave the Emperor $100, he would spend it on clothes. What would **you** spend $100 on? _____

_____

Why?_____

_____
_____
_____
_____

Frog and Toad Are Friends

by Arnold Lobel

Frog and Toad are friends.

When Frog needs companionship, he wakes Toad up from his hibernation so he can play with him.

When Frog is ill, Toad tries as hard as he can to think of a story to cheer him up.

When Toad feels badly about causing Frog a lot of trouble about helping Toad find a button he never really lost, Toad gives Frog his button-covered jacket as a gift.

When Toad thinks he looks funny in his bathing suit, Frog is honest with him — Toad *does* look funny.

And, when Toad is sad because nobody ever sends him any mail, Frog writes him a letter to tell him that he is glad that Toad is his best friend.

Is it in the story?

Read this list:

Toad does not want to get up for Spring.

Frog does not want to get up for Spring.

Toad cannot think of a story to tell Frog.

Frog cannot think of a story to tell Toad.

Toad loses a button.

Frog loses a button.

Toad wears a bathing suit.

Frog wears a bathing suit.

Toad sends Frog a letter.

Frog sends Toad a letter.

Draw a line through the things on this list that do not happen in the story. Then, write the things that do happen on the following lines.

These things happen in the story:

1. _____

   _____

2. _____

   _____

3. _____

   _____

4. _____

   _____

5. _____

   _____

Did Frog Or Toad Say That?

Here are some things that Frog and Toad said in the story. Write Frog or Toad by each thing that was said.

1. "Wake up. It is Spring!"   1._____

2. "Come back again and wake me up at about half past May."   2._____

3. "I hope that if I stand on my head, it will help me to think of a story."   3._____

4. "The whole world is covered with buttons, and not one of them is mine!"   4._____

5. "I am laughing at you, because you **do** look funny in your bathing suit."   5._____

6. "No one has ever sent me a letter."   6._____

7. "Someone may send you a letter today."   7._____

What Happened After This?

Draw a picture of what happened **after** this picture in the story called "A Lost Button."

"A Lost Button"

How Does Toad Feel?

1. In the beginning of the story called "Spring," how does Toad feel about getting up?

   _____

   _____

   _____

   _____

2. How does Toad feel after he bangs his head against the wall to help him think of a story to tell Frog?

   _____

   _____

   _____

3. How does Toad feel when he can't find his button?

   _____

   _____

   _____

4. How does Toad feel in his bathing suit?

   _____

   _____

   _____

5. In the beginning of the story called "The Letter," how does Toad feel as he waits for the mail to come?

   _____

   _____

   _____

Letters For Us!

Write a letter that Frog would enjoy reading. Write things in your letter you think Frog would like to read about.

_____
(date)

Dear Frog,

_____

_____

_____

_____

_____

Your friend,

_____

Write a letter that Toad would enjoy reading. Write things in your letter you think Toad would like to read about.

_____
(date)

Dear Toad,

_____

_____

_____

_____

_____

Your friend,

_____

New Places, Old Faces

Frog and Toad have decided to go for a walk together in the park near your house. On their walk, three things will happen to them. Write what you think Frog and Toad will do when each of these things happen to them.

1. A duck from the park pond splashes water on them.

   Frog will _____

   _____

   Toad will _____

   _____

2. A child almost runs over them with a bicycle.

   Frog will _____

   _____

   Toad will _____

   _____

3. A bird in an elm tree sings a song to them.

   Frog will _____

   _____

   Toad will _____

   _____

Write one more thing that might happen to Frog and Toad in the park. _____

_____

Frog will _____

_____

Toad will _____

_____

40

Friends Can Be Different! (Continued)

In the Toad shape on this page, write how Toad is different from Frog. Color Toad and cut him out. Color the "Friends Can Be Different" banner and cut it out. Paste Frog's hand on one end of the banner and Toad's hand on the other end. They will hold the banner together!

Friends can be different!

I'm different from Frog because

_____

_____

_____

_____

_____

Story Time!

Frog was sick in bed. Toad tried to tell him a story to make him feel better.

Make believe you have a sick friend too. Your sick friend wants to hear a story that will make him or her feel better. Write a story that would make your friend feel better. Draw a picture to go with your story. Read your story and show your picture during a class "Story Time!"

_____

_____

_____

_____

_____

_____

_____

_____

_____

_____

_____

_____

_____

_____

_____

44

It's Not May, It's April!

Frog lied to Toad when he told Toad it was May. Frog wanted Toad to stop hibernating and come outside to play. But now he feels sorry he has lied to his friend and wants to tell Toad the truth.

What could Frog say to Toad? " _____

_____

_____ "

What could Toad answer back? " _____

_____

_____ "

Now, with a partner, rework what you said above into a dialog (conversation) between Frog and Toad. Be sure to pretend you really **are** Frog or Toad! When you have practiced what you wrote, perform the dialog for the class. Use paper bag puppets to help you! (Pages 46-47)

Frog: " _____

_____

_____ "

Toad: " _____

_____

_____ "

Frog: " _____

_____

_____ "

Toad: " _____

_____ "

Frog: " _____

_____ "

Toad: " _____

_____ "

Add more if you need it!

Frog Paper Bag Puppet

46

Toad Paper Bag Puppet

Pick Your Favorite!

There are five stories in **Frog and Toad are Friends:** "Spring," "The Story," "A Lost Button," "A Swim," and "The Letter."

1. Which of the five stories do you like best? _____

_____

Why?_____

_____

_____

_____

2. Which of the stories shows the friendship between Frog and Toad the most? _____

_____

Why?_____

_____

_____

_____

3. Which of the stories would you tell a friend to read first? _____
Why?_____

_____

_____

4. Which of the stories could you draw the best picture for? _____

_____

5. Draw a picture for it on the back of this paper. Share your drawing with the class.

Special Friends

Frog and Toad are special friends.

Who is your special friend? _____

_____

How long has he or she been your
special friend? _____

_____

Where did you meet? _____

_____

What are three things you and your friend like to do together?

1. _____

_____

2. _____

_____

3. _____

_____

What is one thing your friend likes that you don't like? _____

_____

What do you think makes you friends? _____

_____

_____

Do you think your special friend will always be your friend? _____

Why? _____

_____

_____

_____

Ira Sleeps Over

by Bernard Waber

Ira is so excited! He has been invited to spend the night next door at his friend Reggie's house. But his sister reminds him that he has never spent a night without his teddy bear, Tah Tah. He deliberates for a while and decides not to take Tah Tah. At Reggie's house, they play and have a great time. After the boys go to bed, Reggie begins to tell a scary ghost story. He stops in the middle of his story, goes to a drawer, and pulls out *his* teddy bear! Seeing what Reggie does, a happy Ira quickly goes home to bring Tah Tah back to Reggie's house for the night.

SCRAMBLED STORY SENTENCES

Arrange these scrambled story sentences in the order they happen in the story.

1. Reggie gets Foo Foo and goes to bed.
2. Ira's sister reminds Ira that he has never slept without his teddy bear.
3. Ira and Reggie play "office" with rubber stamps.
4. Ira is invited to Reggie's house for the night.
5. Ira gets Tah Tah and goes back to Reggie's house.
6. Reggie tells Ira a ghost story.
7. Ira decides not to take his teddy bear and leaves for Reggie's house.

First _____

_____

Second _____

_____

Third _____

_____

Fourth _____

_____

Fifth _____

_____

Sixth _____

_____

Seventh _____

_____

JUNK!

Reggie showed Ira some "junk" in his room. Do you remember what some of the junk was?

Draw a picture of Reggie's junk. Put at least five junk things from the story in your picture!

HOW DOES IRA FEEL?

1. How does Ira feel when Reggie first asks him to spend the night? _____
   _____
   _____
   _____

2. How does Ira feel when his sister reminds him that he has never slept without his teddy bear? _____
   _____
   _____
   _____

3. How does Ira feel when his sister says Reggie will laugh at him? _____
   _____
   _____

4. How does Ira feel when he finds out that Reggie sleeps with a teddy bear, too? _____
   _____
   _____
   _____

TIME TO WAKE UP!

What do you think will happen in the morning when Ira and Reggie wake up?

_____

_____

_____

_____

_____

Make these Ira and Reggie finger puppets. With a classmate, act out what will happen in the morning. What will Ira and Reggie say to each other? What will they do? After you have practiced with your class partner, put on your "finger puppet play" for the class!

Tah Tah

DIRECTIONS
1. Color and cut out puppets.
2. Paste top and bottom tabs together to form a loop that fits over your finger.

Foo Foo

Ira

Reggie

COME TO MY HOUSE

Reggie planned a fun evening for Ira. Some of the things he planned and they did were seeing Reggie's "junk" collection, having a pillow fight, and telling ghost stories.

If you asked a good friend over to your house for the night, what would you plan to do?

FUN TIME PLANNER

First, we will _____

_____

Second, we will _____

_____

Third, we will _____

_____

Fourth, we will _____

_____

Fifth, we will _____

_____

ALSO:

We may have these snacks_____

_____

We will go to bed at_____o'clock.

We will go to sleep at_____o'clock.

GHOST STORIES!

Read Reggie's ghost story again. What do you think will happen next? Reggie said that the ghost loved to **scare** people. Everything in his story is about how scary the ghost is!

Finish Reggie's story. Remember to keep it scary! When you are finished writing your story, draw a picture of your ghost. Then, take turns with your classmates telling G H O S T stories and showing G H O S T pictures!

Reggie's last words: "Oh, was he scary to look at!"

Your story: _____

_____

_____

_____

_____

_____

_____

_____

_____

_____

_____

IS THIS STORY REAL?

Could this story happen in in real life?_____Why?_____

_____

_____

_____

_____

List three things from the story that could happen in real life.

1._____

_____

2._____

_____

3._____

_____

Has any of these things ever happened to you? _____

Explain your answer. _____

_____

_____

_____

_____

MOM! DAD! SISTER!

1. Ira's mom and dad gave Ira some advice about his teddy bear and his trip to Reggie's house. What did they say? _____

   _____

   _____

2. Ira's sister gave Ira some advice about his teddy bear and his trip to Reggie's house. What did she say? _____

   _____

   _____

3. How was Ira's mom's and dad's advice **different** from his sister's advice?

   _____

   _____

   _____

   _____

   _____

   _____

   _____

4. What advice would **you** give Ira? _____

   _____

   _____

   Why?_____

   _____

TEDDY BEARS ARE *GREAT!*

You have been hired by the owner of a toy store to help sell 1000 teddy bears. The owner likes your ideas and wants you to create an advertising poster for the store window.

Write your ideas in this box. Cut out the box and paste it on a poster with your drawing of a teddy bear. Hang your advertising poster in your classroom!

BUY A TEDDY BEAR TODAY!

Here are three reasons to own a teddy bear:

1._____

_____

2._____

_____

3._____

_____

Teddy bears come in these colors _____

_____

Teddy bears come in these sizes _____

_____

And this great teddy bear only costs _____!

BUY YOURS NOW!

I LOVE MY TEDDY BEAR!

Write a poem about loving a teddy bear. In your poem, be sure to write about why your teddy bear is so special to you. Other things you might want to include in your poem are its name, how long you have had it; what it looks like, things you like to do with it and what would happen to you without it.

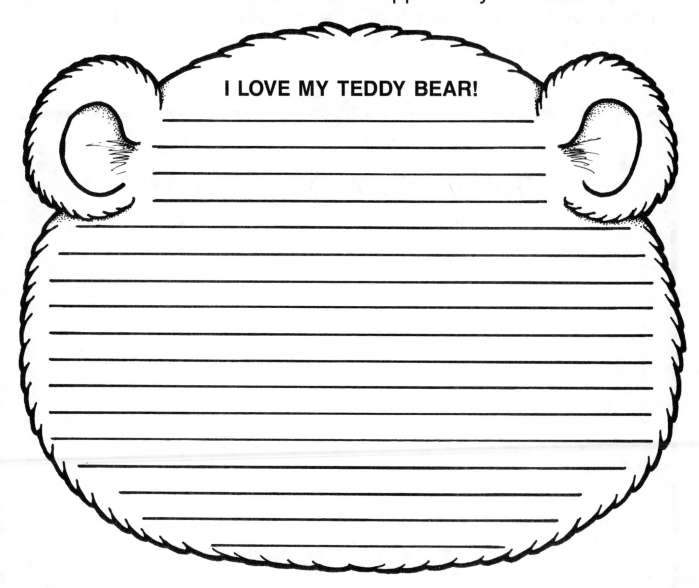

I LOVE MY TEDDY BEAR!

Read your poem to the class! If you would like, "write" music for your poem and sing it as a song!

MY VERY OWN TEDDY BEAR

Materials:
Heavy paper,
scissors, glue
or stapler,
cotton balls or
shredded paper.

Directions:
1. Reproduce
   bear pieces
   on heavy paper.

2. Color, cut out
   and glue or
   staple 3/4 of
   the way around
   bear.

3. Stuff with
   cotton balls
   or shredded
   paper.

4. Staple or
   glue closed
   rest of
   bear.

5. Add button eyes
   and a ribbon or
   paper bow!

MY VERY OWN TEDDY BEAR

BUT MY SISTER SAID...

1. Ira's sister kept trying to make Ira feel that it was not a good idea to take Tah Tah over to Reggie's house for the night. Why do you think she did that? _____

   _____

   _____

   _____

2. Do you think Ira listened to what his sister said?_____
   How do you know? _____

   _____

   _____

3. Ira's mom and dad kept trying to make Ira feel that taking Tah Tah to Reggie's house was a good idea. Why do you think they did that? _____

   _____

   _____

4. Do you think Ira listened to what his parents said? _____
   How do you know? _____

   _____

   _____

5. If your little brother or sister was going to sleep over at a friend's house like Ira did, would you tell him or her to take a special sleep toy? _____
   Why?_____

   _____

   _____

   _____

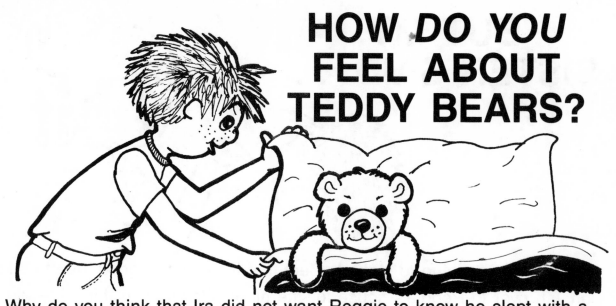

HOW *DO YOU* FEEL ABOUT TEDDY BEARS?

1. Why do you think that Ira did not want Reggie to know he slept with a Teddy Bear named Tah Tah? _____

   _____

   _____

2. Before Ira went to Reggie's house, he tried to ask Reggie how he felt about Teddy Bears two times. Reggie didn't seem to hear his questions. Do you think Reggie heard Ira's questions? _____
   Why?_____

   _____

3. Why do you think Reggie might not want to answer a question about teddy bears?_____

   _____

   _____

4. Were you surprised when Reggie pulled a teddy bear out of his drawer?
   _____ Do you think Ira was surprised? _____
   Why?_____

   _____

   _____

5. Is there anything you don't want your friends to know about you?_____
   Why?_____

   _____

   _____

The Velveteen Rabbit

by Margery Williams Bianco

A beautiful Velveteen Rabbit peeks out of a stocking on Christmas morning. A boy plays with it for a short time, then relegates it to the toy closet. While in the toy closet, the Velveteen Rabbit learns from the Skin Horse that if a child loves him for a long, long time, he could become real. And the Velveteen Rabbit wants very much to be REAL. One night the boy sleeps with the Velveteen Rabbit and the friendship begins. The boy and the Velveteen Rabbit go everywhere and do everything together. The Velveteen Rabbit is deeply loved and real to the boy. But the boy gets scarlet fever and many of his things are set out to be burned, including the Velveteen Rabbit. A Fairy rescues the Velveteen Rabbit, takes him to a rabbit warren, and kisses him. Her magic makes him real to the real rabbits of the warren *and* everyone!

Story Pictures

Color these pictures of things that happen in **The Velveteen Rabbit.** Cut each picture out and paste each picture in the order that it happened in the story. Use the STORY PICTURE FRAME.

66

THE VELVETEEN RABBIT
Story Picture Frame

TEACHER: Use this frame for all story pictures in this book.

Color inside the frame borders. Paste story pictures inside frame in the order that they happen.

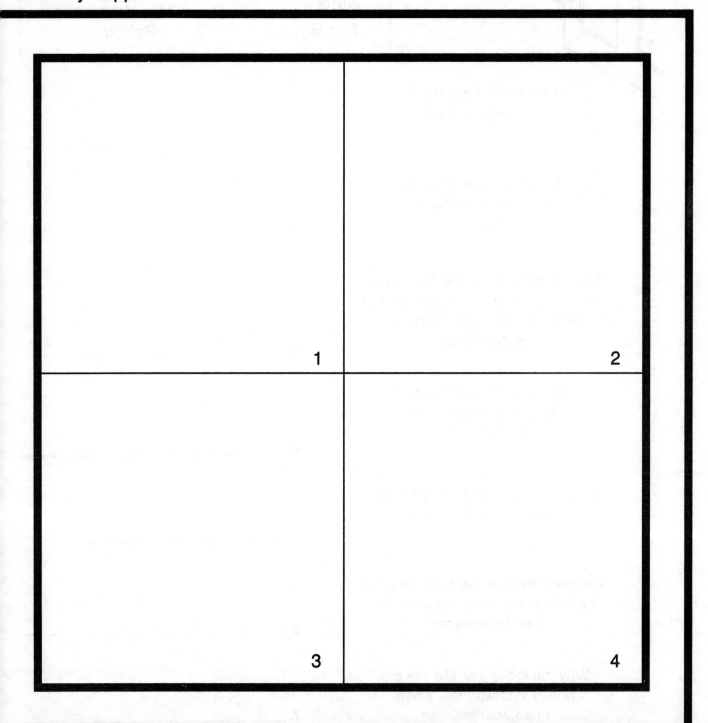

Who said that?

Read the names in the word box. Write each name next to what each character said.

The Skin Horse	Rabbits
The Doctor	The Fairy
Nana	The Velveteen
The Boy	Rabbit

I am Real! I am Real!
The Boy said so!

1. _____

You must have your old
bunny! Fancy all that fuss
for a toy!

2. _____

When a child loves you for a long,
long time, not just to play with, but
REALLY loves you, then you
become Real.

3. _____

He doesn't smell right!
He isn't a rabbit at all!
He isn't real!

4. _____

Why, it's a mass of scarlet fever
germs! Burn it at once.

5. _____

You were Real to the Boy because
he loved you. Now you shall be
Real to everyone.

6. _____

Why, he looks just like my old
bunny that was lost when
I had scarlet fever!

7. _____

How does he feel?

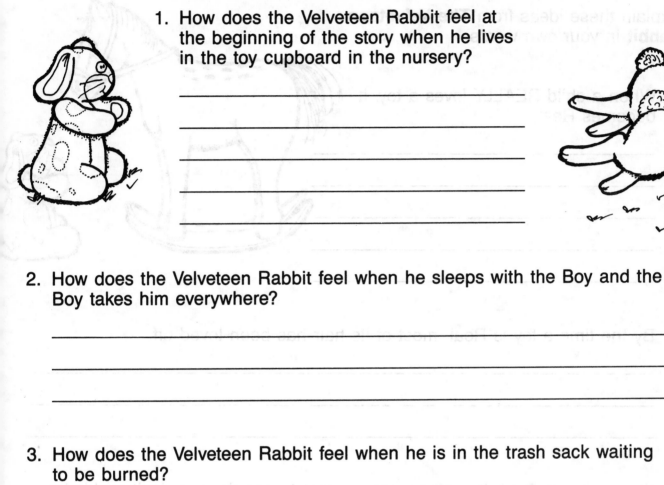

1. How does the Velveteen Rabbit feel at the beginning of the story when he lives in the toy cupboard in the nursery?

_____

_____

_____

_____

_____

2. How does the Velveteen Rabbit feel when he sleeps with the Boy and the Boy takes him everywhere?

_____

_____

_____

3. How does the Velveteen Rabbit feel when he is in the trash sack waiting to be burned?

_____

_____

_____

4. How does the Velveteen Rabbit feel when the nursery magic Fairy makes him Real and he can hop by himself?

_____

_____

_____

In your words . . . .

Explain these ideas from **The Velveteen Rabbit** in your own words.

1. When a child REALLY loves a toy, it becomes Real.

   _____

   _____

   _____

   _____

2. By the time a toy is Real, most of its hair has been loved off.

   _____

   _____

   _____

3. Once a toy is Real, it can't be ugly, except to people who don't understand.

   _____

   _____

   _____

4. Once a toy becomes Real, it can't become unreal again.

   _____

   _____

   _____

70

What would you have done?

The Boy had scarlet fever. When he got better, the doctor ordered all the toys and books that has been with the Boy in his bed to be burned. The Velveteen Rabbit went into the sack of things to burn.

The Boy slept that night in a different room, with a splendid, new bunny. But he didn't think much about anything except going to the seaside in the morning. The Velveteen Rabbit seemed to be forgotten.

What would *you* have done in the Boy's place?

_____

_____

_____

_____

_____

_____

_____

_____

_____

_____

_____

_____

Finger Puppets!

Make these finger puppets and act out a part of the story to the class. You may choose any part of the story you would like and work in groups!

DIRECTIONS
1. Color and cut out puppets.
2. Paste top and bottom tabs together to form a loop that fits around your finger.
3. Now you are ready to act out a part of the story.

Nana

Real Rabbit

Boy

Fairy

Velveteen Rabbit

Skin Horse

Look at my rabbit!

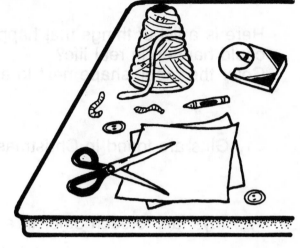

Write some words from the story that tell what the Velveteen Rabbit looked like at the beginning of the story.

1. Color of his coat _____

2. Color of his ear lining _____

3. Spots or no spots on his coat_____

4. Color of his eyes _____

5. Fat or thin _____

6. Kind of material the rabbit is made from_____

_____

7. Number of legs _____

8. Kind of whiskers_____

9. Size _____ (The rabbit fit inside a Christmas _____ .)

Use the information you wrote to make a Velveteen Rabbit of your own. You may use construction paper, crayons, paint, material scraps, yarn, buttons, cotton, or other materials you might think of.

Make a class bulletin board of Velveteen Rabbits! (Teacher, you may want to make a bulletin board "mantle" and have students display their rabbits in stockings hung on the mantle.)

What could happen?

Here is a list of things that happened in **The Velveteen Rabbit.** What things could happen in real life?
Color the rabbit shape next to each thing that *could* happen.

1. Gifts are found in Christmas stockings.

2. Toys talk to each other in a child's room.

3. A woman called Nana cleans up toys.

4. A child sleeps with a stuffed animal.

5. A child plays with a stuffed animal outside.

6. Rabbits talk to a stuffed animal and the stuffed animal talks back.

7. A child gets scarlet fever.

8. A Velveteen Rabbit cries a real tear.

9. A flower turns into the nursery magic Fairy.

10. A stuffed animal changes into a real animal.

My Favorite Toy

- What is your favorite toy? _____
  _____

- What is so special about this toy? _____
  _____

- Does it have a name? _____

- Who gave it to you? _____

- How long have you had it? _____

- What is one thing you like to do with your favorite toy? _____
  _____

Now, it's your favorite toy's turn to talk! Pretend your toy is giving the answers!
Fill in *all* the blanks.

1. My name is_____.

2. My favorite person is _____
   because _____
   _____.

3. The thing that makes me happiest is when _____
   _____
   _____.

4. The thing that makes me saddest is when _____
   _____
   _____.

5. If I could have one wish, I would wish that _____
   _____
   _____.

Show Time!

Pretend *you* are your favorite toy. Write a paragraph about yourself! Use your answers on the "My Favorite Toy" page to help you.

Hi! My name is _____

and I belong to _____ .

I love my owner because _____

_____ .

I am happiest when _____

_____

I wish that_____

_____ .

Cut out your finished paragraph. Bring your favorite toy to school and attach your paragraph to it. Make a FAVORITE TOY SHOW with the other students in your class. Take your toy in front of the class. Pretend *you* are the toy and tell the class about yourself! (Use your paragraph to help you.)

How Toys Become Real

The title of the book you just read is **The Velveteen Rabbit or How Toys Become Real.** Do you like the way the Velveteen

Rabbit became real in this story?_____

Why? _____

_____

Now it's your turn to write your own story about how a toy becomes real.

Things to do:

1. Think of a way that a toy might become real.

2. Write a story about how the toy becomes real.

3. Draw pictures to go with your story. Be sure to draw a picture of the toy before it becomes real *and* after it becomes real.

4. Make a nice cover for your book.

5. Use staples, brads, or yarn to put your book together.

6. Read your book to the class!

Write your idea about how a toy might become real here: _____

_____

_____

I like . . .

Which one of the characters in the story do you like best? _____
Why? _____
_____

Which of the characters in the story do you like least? _____
Why? _____
_____

Make an award for your favorite character. Fill in the blanks on the ribbon.
Color the ribbon and cut it out. Put the ribbon in your **Favorite Characters**
memory book. (See page 2)

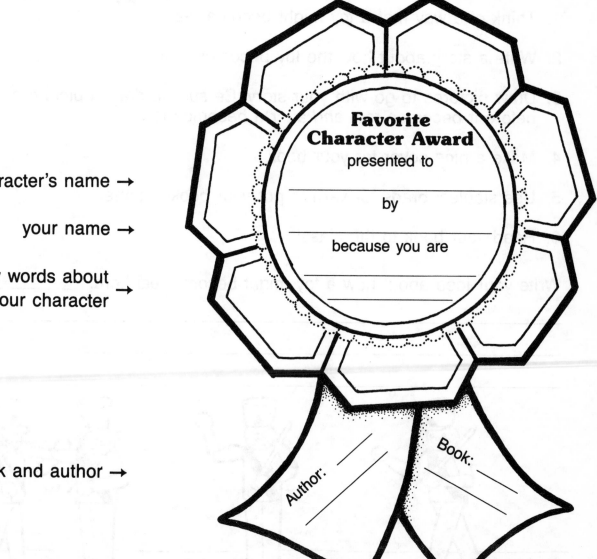

character's name →

your name →

a few words about
your character →

book and author →

**Favorite
Character Award**
presented to
_____
by
_____
because you are
_____
_____

Author: _____
Book: _____

Real or Unreal?

The Velveteen Rabbit wanted to be real. He finally became real by the end of the story.

1. What do you think *real* means? _____
   _____
   _____
   _____

2. Was there ever *anything* that you thought was real that really wasn't?_____

3. What was it? _____
   _____.

4. When did it stop being real to you? _____
   _____
   _____.

5. Do you think it could ever be real to you again?_____ Why? _____
   _____
   _____.

6. Do you think growing up has anything to do with not believing some things are real anymore?_____ Why? _____
   _____
   _____
   _____.

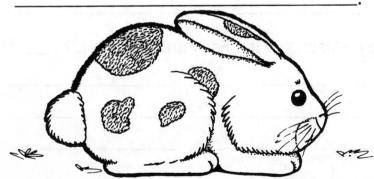

EVALUATION: Activity 3

♥ Love is REAL!

The Boy loved the Velveteen Rabbit very much. Why do you think he did?

_____

_____

_____

Do you have a stuffed animal that

you love? _____ What is it? _____

What is its name? _____

Why do you love your stuffed animal? _____

_____

_____

_____

Does your love for your stuffed animal make it real to you? _____

Why? _____

_____

_____

_____

Can stuffed animals ever be real? _____ Why? _____

_____

_____

_____

_____

Would you like your stuffed animal to be kissed by the Fairy and made real? _____

Why? _____

_____

_____

The Whingdingdilly

by Bill Peet

Scamp is not happy with his life as a dog. He wants to be a horse so he can be admired by all, especially his owner, a boy named Orvie. So, disenchanted with who he is, Scamp runs away deep into the forest. There he encounters Zildy, a witch who turns him into a whingdingdilly, a creature that is a conglomeration of animals. But Scamp is not happy as a whingdingdilly either. He is disliked by farmers and captured by a great showman who puts him on display. Finally Zildy, angered because the whingdingdilly trampled her tulips, turns Scamp back into a dog. Happy to be a dog once again, Scamp runs home to a joyous reunion with Orvie!

THIS IS A WHINGDINGDILLY!

Fill in these blanks to describe the whingdingdilly.

1. a hump like a _____

2. hind legs like a _____ with _____ stripes

3. tail like a _____

4. squarish brown spots like a _____

5. big feet and front legs like an _____

6. a nose like a _____

7. ears like an _____

8. horns like a _____

SCRAMBLED STORY SENTENCES

Here are five sentences explaining five things that happen in **The Whingdingdilly.** Write the sentences in the order they happen in the story.

1. Zildy changes Scamp into a whingdingdilly.
2. Scamp feels he is lucky to be a dog and have Orvie.
3. Scamp wants to be a horse like Palomar.
4. Zildy changes the whingdingdilly into Scamp.
5. C.J. Pringle captures the whingdingdilly.

Write the sentences in order here.

1. _____

_____

2. _____

_____

3. _____

_____

4. _____

_____

5. _____

_____

HOW DOES SCAMP FEEL?

Be sure to EXPLAIN each answer.

1. How does Scamp feel at the beginning of the story when he is watching Palomar? _____

    _____

    _____

    _____

2. How does Scamp feel in the middle of the story when he is the whing-dingdilly? _____

    _____

    _____

    _____

3. How does Scamp feel at the end of the story when he is a dog again and Orvie is playing with him?_____

    _____

    _____

    _____

ROWF! ROWF!

At the end of the story, Orvie asked Scamp where he had been. But all Scamp could answer was, "Rowf! Rowf!"

Pretend you **can** talk to Orvie! And pretend **you** are Scamp! Tell Orvie what happened to you in the order that it happened. Remember, **you** are telling the story as if you are Scamp!

_____

_____

_____

_____

_____

_____

_____

_____

_____

_____

_____

_____

_____

MY PET!

You wake up and find the whingdingdilly asleep outside your window. You would love to have it as a pet! Now the whingdingdilly is starting to wake up.

1. What will you do first when the whingdingdilly wakes up? _____

   _____

   _____

   _____

2. What will the whingdingdilly do when it wakes up? _____

   _____

   _____

   _____

3. Does the whingdingdilly want to be your pet? _____
   Why?_____

   _____

   _____

4. What is one thing you two will do together? _____

   _____

   _____

5. What will your friends say about your new pet? _____

   _____

   _____

6. What will your parents say about your new pet? _____

   _____

I'M HUNGRY!

Your pet whingdingdilly is **very** hungry. The only problem is, you don't quite know what to feed your pet because it is many animals in one.

Scamp

1. What are some kinds of food you **might** feed your whingdingdilly? _____
   _____
   _____
   _____

2. What foods do you think your whingdingdilly will like best? _____
   _____
   Why?_____
   _____

3. It is mealtime. What have you decided to feed your pet? _____
   _____
   _____

4. How will you serve it? _____
   _____
   _____

5. Does your whingdingdilly like the meal? _____
   Why?_____
   _____
   _____

SAME OR DIFFERENT?

Scamp thought his life would change if he could just be different than what he was.

1. When Scamp was a whingdingdilly, did he feel the same as he did when he was an unhappy dog? _____ How or why? _____

_____

_____

2. Was his life any different when he was a whingdingdilly? _____ How or why? _____

_____

_____

3. Was his life the same as it was at the beginning of the story after Zildy turned him back into Scamp? _____ How or why? _____

_____

_____

4. Was his life any different than it was at the beginning of the story after Zildy turned him back into Scamp? _____ How or why? _____

_____

_____

5. Did Scamp's life as a dog change at the end of the story or did Scamp change the way he thought about himself? _____

_____

_____

SAD AND HAPPY

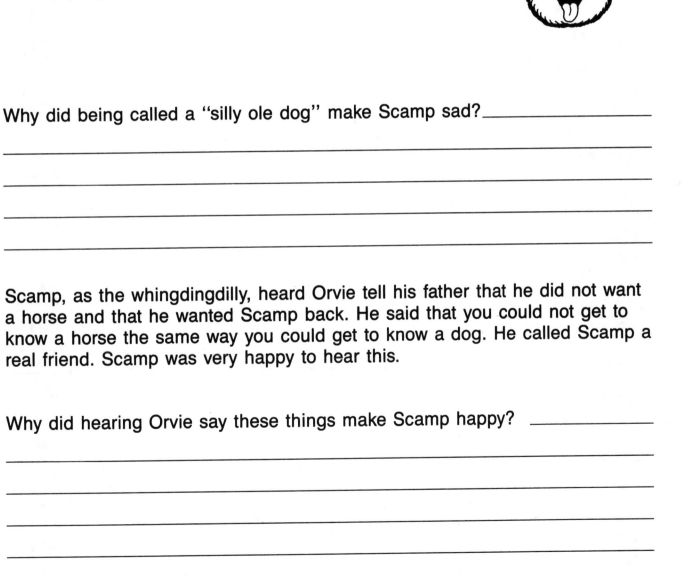

Orvie called Scamp a "silly ole dog" when Scamp pretended to be Palomar. Being called a silly ole dog made Scamp very sad. It was more than he could bear, and Scamp ran away.

Why did being called a "silly ole dog" make Scamp sad?_____

_____

_____

_____

_____

Scamp, as the whingdingdilly, heard Orvie tell his father that he did not want a horse and that he wanted Scamp back. He said that you could not get to know a horse the same way you could get to know a dog. He called Scamp a real friend. Scamp was very happy to hear this.

Why did hearing Orvie say these things make Scamp happy? _____

_____

_____

_____

_____

MAGIC WORDS!

You and your classmates are going to make a magic words book! Complete the dictionary page below and give it to your teacher. Your teacher will put all the class pages together for a MAGIC WORDS BOOK!

Name: _____

Magic Words: _____

_____

The best way to say the words: _____

_____

What happens when the words are said: _____

_____

_____

How to "undo" the magic: _____

_____

Picture of magic happening:

A WHAT?

Create your own creature that is the only one of its kind in the whole world. You will work in a group of three to four students.

First 1: Each group member will create one part of the creature's body on a 12″x18″ piece of construction paper. For example, one person will make just the head, while others will make the front legs, middle body, back legs, or tail (if these are body parts your creature has). The creature can be assembled on a large piece of paper or, if you wish, you may make a model instead (paper mache, tubes, yarn, etc.).

Write your group's names and assignments here.

1. _____
          name of group member

           _____
                    part(s) to make

2. _____

           _____

           _____

3. _____

           _____

4. _____

           _____

Second: Together, the group will decide what information will go on the creature information plaque on page 92. When it is filled in, cut it out and attach it to your creature with paste, staples, yarn, or brads.

CREATURE INFORMATION PLAQUE

Fill in the information needed. Color the plaque and cut it out. Attach it to your creature!

_____

Creature's name

Age:_____   Height:_____   Weight:_____

Where it lives: _____

_____

What it eats: _____

_____

What it drinks: _____

_____

What it wears: _____

_____

What it loves to do:_____

_____

What to do if you see it: _____

_____

_____

_____

YOU ARE SPECIAL!

This story is about learning that everyone can be special. At the beginning of the story, Scamp did not think he was special the way he was. At the end of the story, Scamp knew he was special, just the way he was. What made him change the way he felt?

_____

_____

_____

Do you think you are special just the way you are? _____
Why?_____

_____

_____

What are three things you like about yourself?

1. _____
   Why?_____

2. _____
   Why?_____

3. _____
   Why?_____

What is one thing you do not like about yourself?_____

_____

Why?_____

_____

Do you want to change it? _____ Why? _____

_____

Can you change it?_____ If yes, how? _____

_____

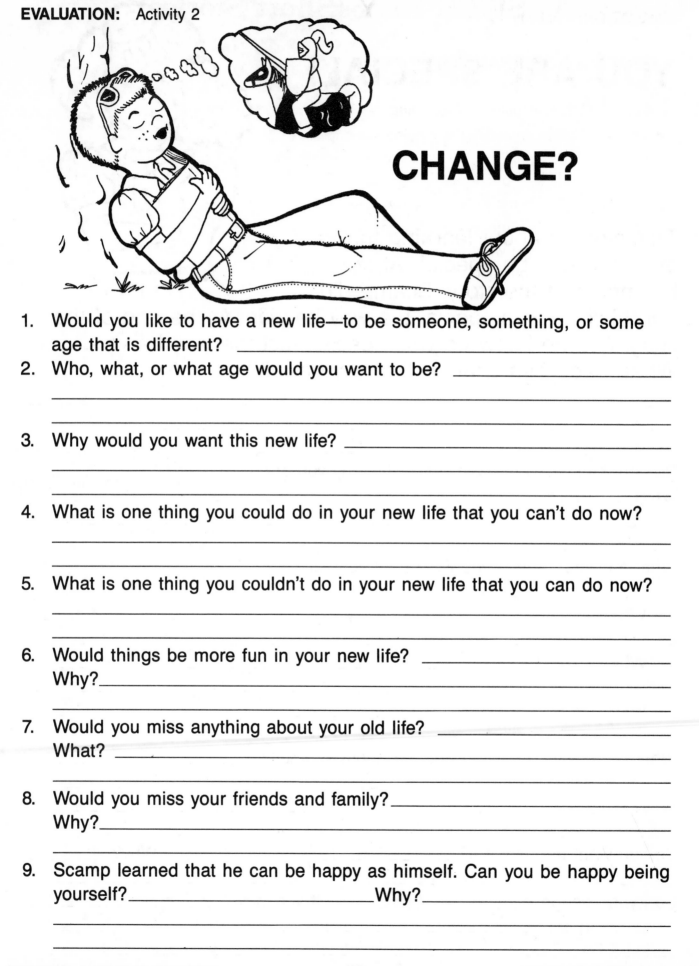

CHANGE?

1. Would you like to have a new life—to be someone, something, or some age that is different? _____

2. Who, what, or what age would you want to be? _____
_____
_____

3. Why would you want this new life? _____
_____
_____

4. What is one thing you could do in your new life that you can't do now?
_____
_____

5. What is one thing you couldn't do in your new life that you can do now?
_____
_____

6. Would things be more fun in your new life? _____
Why?_____
_____

7. Would you miss anything about your old life? _____
What? _____
_____

8. Would you miss your friends and family?_____
Why?_____
_____

9. Scamp learned that he can be happy as himself. Can you be happy being yourself?_____Why?_____
_____

94

ANSWER KEY (Short Stories)

BEDTIME FOR FRANCES

K-1   1) 4   2) 5   3) 2   4) 1   5) 3

K-2   Picture should be something like a chair and a bathrobe.

C-1   "Father, something is moving the curtains,"

        "I'm scared,"   "May I sleep with you?", etc.

        "Frances, go to sleep,"   "It is the wind,"

        "It is your job to sleep," etc.

C-2   1) "He is a friendly tiger," etc.

        2) "Ask him what he wants," etc.

        3) "Get somebody to help you watch," etc.

        4) "That is the wind's job," etc.

An-1   tiger,   giant,   something coming through crack in ceiling

THE EMPEROR'S NEW CLOTHES

K-1   **across:** 2) councillor   4) weaver   7) wardrobe   9) trousers
        10) procession   12) train   13) minister   15) position   16) court
        17) cunning   18) dignity

        down: 1) loom   2) chamberlains   3) cloak   5) Emperor
        6) empire   8) post   9) trickster   11) canopy   14) innocent

K-2   The tricksters fooled the Emperor and the other people into believing their special cloth was real, etc.

C-2   1) happy with his extensive wardrobe, etc.

        2) confused, but afraid to be seen as unfit or stupid, etc.

        3) ashamed, but felt he must carry on, etc.

An-2   1) caring too much about how one looks

        2) dishonest   3) very honest in what one says

FROG AND TOAD ARE FRIENDS

K-1   things that happened
        (all others should be crossed out)

        Toad . . . spring
        Toad . . . story . . . Frog.
        Toad . . . button.
        Toad . . . bathing suit.
        Frog . . . letter.

K-2   1) Frog   2) Toad   3) Toad   4) Toad
        5) Frog   6) Toad   7) Frog

C-1   Toad gives his jacket (covered with buttons) to a very happy Frog.

C-2   1) tired, etc.   2) miserable, goes to bed, etc.   3) angry, etc.

        4) that he looks funny, etc.   5) sad, etc.

ANSWER KEY (Short Stories cont.)

IRA SLEEPS OVER

K-1   first-4   second-2   third-7   fourth-3   fifth-6   sixth-1   seventh-5

C-1   1) Ira is thrilled, etc.   2) Ira is unsure about his evening ahead, etc.

3) Ira believes her, is nervous, etc.

4) Ira feels at "peace" and very happy, etc.

An-2   Ira's mom and dad said to take the teddy bear if he wanted to, etc.

Ira's sister said not to take the teddy bear because Reggie would laugh at him, etc.

Ira's mom and dad just wanted Ira to be comfortable and felt that Reggie would not laugh at him.

THE VELVETEEN RABBIT

K-1   1) Christmas tree   2) Rabbit, Boy, garden   3) Rabbit, trash bag

4) REAL Velveteen Rabbit

K-2   1) The Velveteen Rabbit   2) Nana   3) The Skin House

4) Rabbits   5) The Doctor   6) The Fairy   7) The Boy

C-1   1) lonely, sad, shy, wants to be loved, etc.

2) happy to be loved, etc.

3) very unhappy, etc.

4) wonderful, etc.

An-1   1) spotted brown and white   2) pink   3) spots   4) black
5) fat   6) velveteen   7) two   8) thread   9) small or medium; stocking

An-2   **could happen:** 1, 3, 4, 5, 7

THE WHINGDINGDILLY

K-1   1) camel   2) camel, zebra   3) zebra   4) giraffe   5) elephant

6) rhinoceros   7) elephant   8) reindeer

K-2   3, 1, 5, 4, 2

C-1   1) sad,   wants to be a horse and admired like Palomar

2) sad, uncomfortable as the whingdingdilly

3) happy to be himself and back with Orvie